Brain Dump

Also by William N. Duncan

It's Full of Stars

The River II *(with Jeffrey G. Ludlow)*

Brain Dump

black edition

William N. Duncan

1194793 Ontario Inc. • Aurora

First published by 1194793 Ontario Inc, Aurora 2019

Copyright © 2018 William Duncan

Any similarity to real persons, living or dead, is coincidental and not intended by the author, although some characters and events in this book are real.

3 5 7 9 bd 10 8 6 4 2

Design/photograph/images/ "art" work/scans by Duncan

First edition (black)

ISBN-13:   978-0-9731728-6-7 (pbk.)

ATTENTION SCHOOLS AND BUSINESSES:
1194793 Ontario Inc. books are available at quantity discounts with bulk purchase for educational, business, or sales promotional use. For information, please contact the publisher.

Contents

Preface

In a similar fashion to Douglas Coupland's "Bit Rot", I give you *Brain Dump*, the *black edition*. For a more detailed explanation as to why I do this, refer to the preface in, "It's full of Stars" (ISBN: 978-0-9731728-0-5).

These prose have been presented in chronological order. Most of the writing is naked and raw in its first cut version with minimal, if any, editing. These musings are driven out of feelings or imagery that takes hold of me unannounced, usually through the night or in the early waking hours (sounds cliché but it's true). My goal is to capture the mood or feeling of the experience, but I have found the words (or more accurately my limited vocabulary) fail to convey what I had hoped. So I gather and present them in this form on the off-chance that the reader may see something that resonates with them. If not, try reading a different piece, or abandon this book altogether. I am not one to spell things out and enjoy entertainment that leaves the meaning open to interpretation, so that's the way I write. Everything that follows is open to interpretation. Not all of these prose are dark, some start in a dark place and end up in the light, others are and remain black because they need to be. Enjoy, be kind, and comment if you like.

This edition contains a special *Bonus Material* section at the end.

Aurora, January 2018

Black

William N. Duncan

Original cover concept art, circa 2002.

A DAY in the LIFE
(day in day out)

Get up at the same time
Same morning get ready routine
Listen to the same radio station
Same breakfast
Leave at the same time
Same drive
Arrive at the same time
Drink the same coffee
Walk the same route
Sit in the same chair
Stare at the same screen
Work on the same stuff
Listen to the same patter
Lunch at the same desk
Time drags in the same way
Leave at the same time
Same drive
Arrive at the same time
Go to bed at the same time
Sleep
Get up at the same time ...

All these "things" are
significant.
artifacts from a youth.
everybody has their walls
     ''   ''   '' monkeys
     ''   ''   '' $\frac{2}{2}$

(untitled fragment 7)

Of flying monkeys, rainbows and walls.
These things are ... essential.
Artifacts from someone's youth.

Everybody has their monkeys.
Everybody has their rainbows.
Everybody has their walls.

Find your own,
and ask them why?

GRENDEL

The beast has returned.
It crawls up out of the mire.
Sharp talons scraping at the dirt,
as it heaves itself out onto the land.

Grendel, but this Grendel feeds on emotions
not flesh and blood.
It survives to torment, and upset,
spewing forth its own insecurities.

Hulking about in its dark cave,
this place has remained black since the light left.
Demanding notice and reassurance,
the centre of its world.
Unyielding in its resolve to be pitiful.

Unprovoked and ill-thought verbal attacks.
Unwilling to pull itself up and out.
Content to sit, day to day, in self-pity
and inflict its misery on others.

The beast is slowly wearing its time down.
Happy to be miserable as long as it can drag others down.
Constantly making excuses for its lot,
never taking responsibility for its own future.

Oh! Cry me a river, woe.

cont'd

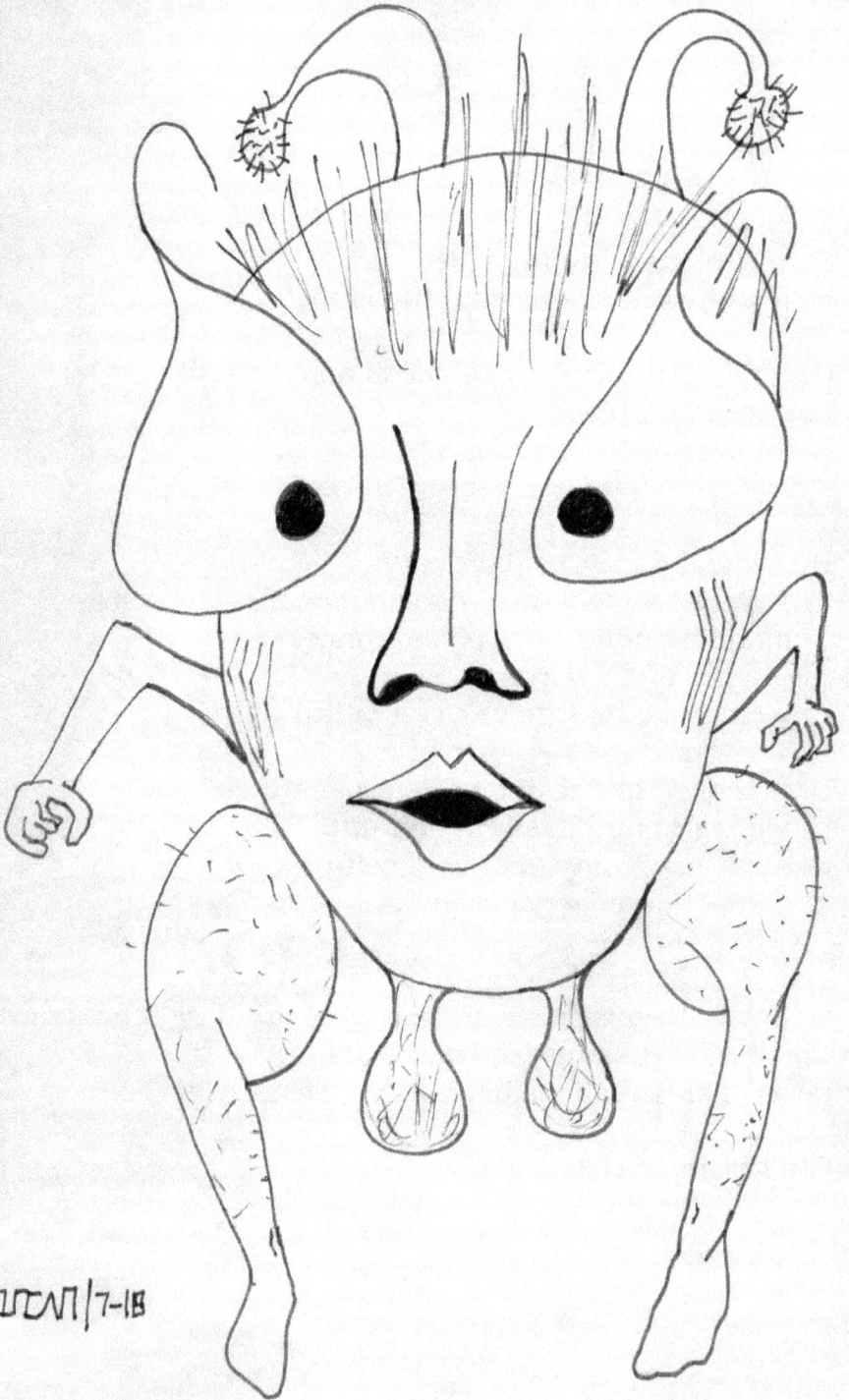

Grendel ...

No longer can it see any light,
no spark of hope, no shine.
Not only in itself, but all around.
Unable to make its way through the forest to
the tree line
to get a new glimpse, of how it could be on the
other side.

Blind now forever, unless by some miracle ...

But, miracles are hard to come by these days.

ON LEAVING[1]

It's closing in again
this cube, my home.
For days now, I've watched the trains pass.
One of these days I'll hitch a ride.

Far, far away; wherever the tracks lead.
Just thought I'd come by
one last time, satisfy my need
to say goodbye.

Often, I've sat in the car,
the monotony of the drive
lulls me to dreaming of places afar
where I could possibly feel alive.

My farewells have been made,
the ones that count.
All the reasons begin to fade
removing my fear and any doubt.

RELEASE

Crawling through the fog and haze of everyday existence.
Learning the daily drudge by rote.
I feel myself slipping... drifting in and out.

Some part is missing, a hole in its place,
filled with emptiness and darkness.

Something essential to the machine has been misplaced.
Something required to give this meaning,
some reason for existing, some reason for being.

Constantly seeking answers to questions unspoken.
Released from the incessant dialogue in my head, to the ether
with hopes that some divine manifestation will reward me
with answers.

Every day now, I feel like I'm in a daze.
The endless drone of life,
routines, unwavering and constant in their monotony.
Searching for some meaning, some reason to continue.
Feelings brought upon, not by melancholy, but by boredom.
What kind of a waste is this short time here?
What reason do I have to continue?
When I'm done, does the light just go out,
then it means something because it means nothing.
I no longer need to ponder these questions.

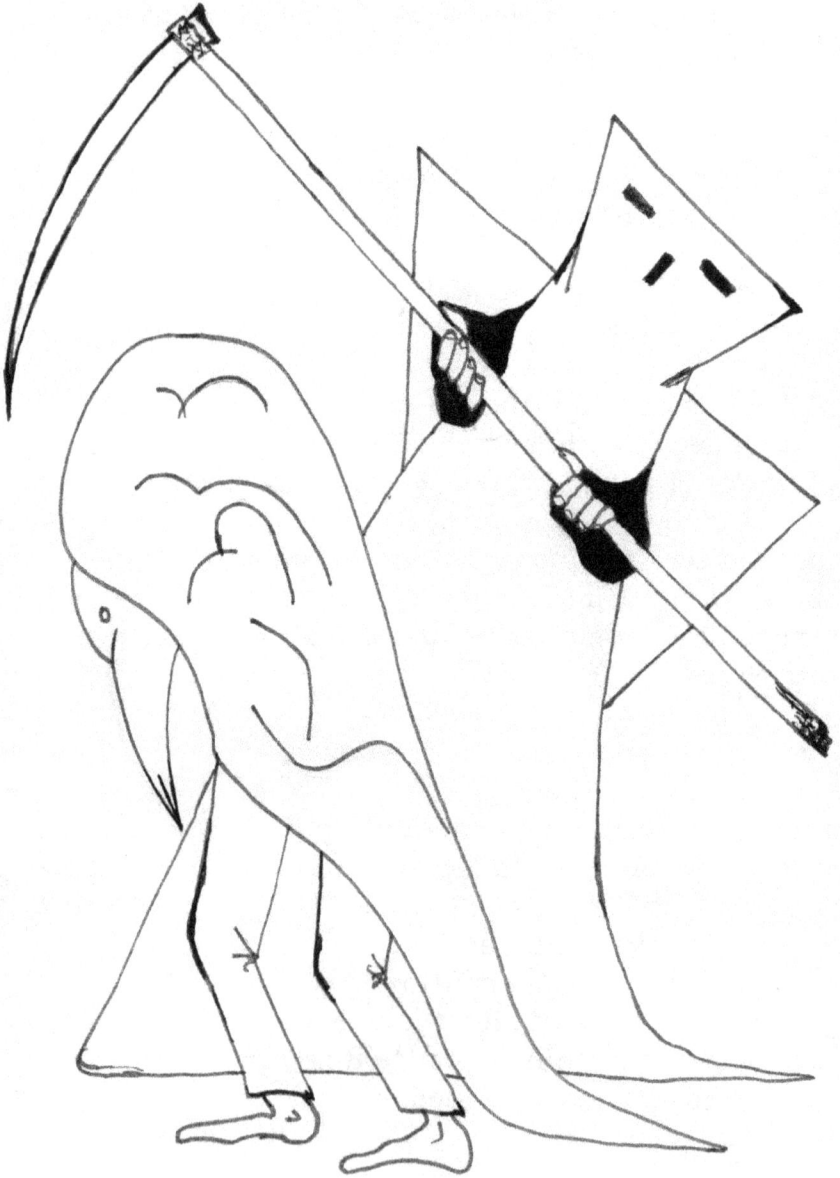

IMAGE²

My head fills with movie clips and sound bites from the
radio.
When I listen, the songs drive out feelings.
This is how things should be.
Somewhere I have been misled and pushed down the wrong
path.

I have visions, images that reoccur, more than just
coincidence.
My visionary emotions pull stronger than the real ones.
The scenes inside my head stir me more than the world I see.

This world is gray and uneventful,
filled with the just-getting-by crowd.
Day after day drones on,
numbed by my commitment to responsibility.

How can this be, my imaginary world seems more real than
the *real* world.
One day maybe I'll wake to find things reversed.
Now I belong where I am, things will then seem right,
living *the* life, and dreaming of the mundane.

I wonder if there is a portal, a bridge, somewhere,
a means to cross over to this other place.
Should I search, should I try?
And what if I find it?

Do I even get a choice?

ISOLATION

Sitting by my window, looking out,
hoar frost covers everything.
White covered hills that stretch on forever.
A cold wind blowing under the door.

The door is locked now
no one would make the journey now.
Endless knocking and rattling
brought on by the relentless winds.

The season of sleep and cold
nothing new can start or take hold.
Movements are minimal and scarce,
every action is laboured and deliberate.

What trees I can see, are bare and skeletal.
Foliage long stripped to bits,
branches left unstable and brittle
and trunks painted white in the drifts.

The sun burns its way through the haze
of these long and monotonous days.
Promising life for the future
for all lonesome and solitary creatures.

The limitless blackness of these winter nights,
submit to my concentrated gaze.
Offering up stars and their points of light
that dance before me in an endless maze.

HOUSE[1]

Standing on the road across from your house
I had to stop and say goodbye.
I'm leaving today,
got to catch that train and head for the coast.
You know, that same train I always talk about.

How many days and evenings did we sit on the porch?
Watching the world go by,
watching the seasons change.
Waiting for a sign, something significant.

The train doesn't run by here as often anymore.
There may not be another chance to catch it.
Today I have decided, this is the one for me.
Wave to me and wish me well.

The only house on this stretch of road for miles.

One day I'll catch another train,
head back here,
stand in this same spot,
and look at this house once again, through different eyes.

The DARK DAYS

The dark days are the worst.
Closed in,
dim, dull, gray light.
Suffocating closeness.
Slow monotonous drum beat.
Gunmetal hammer beating on stones.
Frustration and anxiety sucked out of me
like strands of a rope.
Looped rope, swinging back and forth.
Slowly revolving stars
and unfortunate destinations.
Senses scrubbed bare
left open to the elements.
Weathered and beaten
until reduced to jelly and pulp.
Distorted faces looking in,
predatory, accusatory, self-serving.
This silence is louder than any other.
Constant, relentless, ever-present screaming.
Drowning in this endless emptiness.

One of my turns.

Let's hope tomorrow brings the sun.

ON SEEING MOUNTAINS

Read the space between my lines
superimposed images of the beginning.
Carbon copies made real
send the meaning held within.

So many turns that fell upon themselves,
circular paths that start and end.
Ancient animal skulls
speaking wisdom seldom heard
and never made real.

Your enemy hides here
not there, not with the stranger.
You've seen that face before
stretched thin covering the familiar.

You are not always invited
you cannot spend your currency here.

Flames, burn, flare, and sputter out,
use the moonlight as a guide.
Mistress tonight, hammered hard and left to the dark,
walk obliviously to the order.

Painted walls slough off ages.
Should the trail lead there,
the pieces don't quite fit,
given a second chance to make it stay.

Moving inside the sphere, impenetrable loneliness.
A shell of hardening layers,
flat, barren and motionless,
spread thin in its execution.

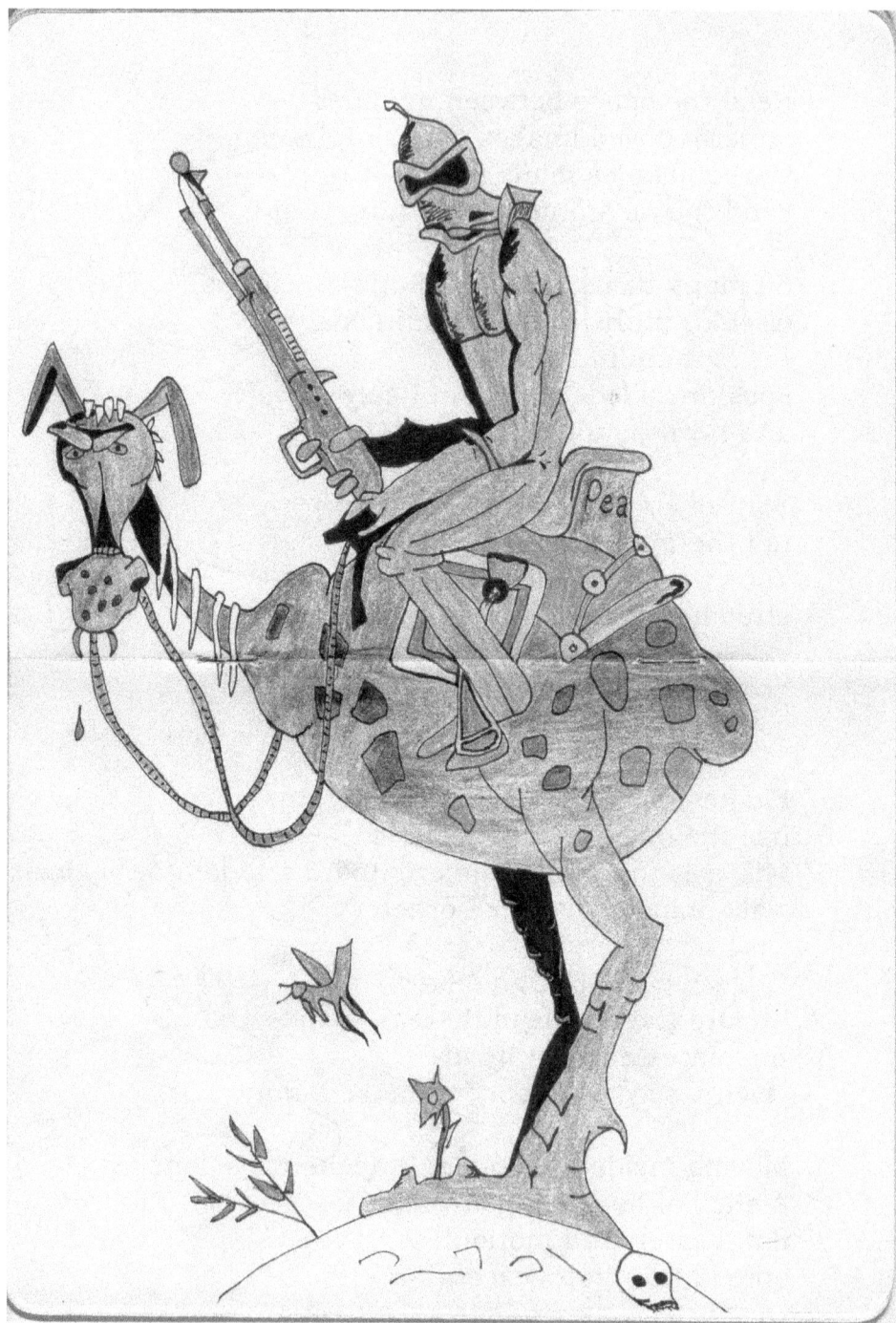

VISITING DAY

Where are you from?
The same place as you.
Should we go there now?
If not now, then when?

I like to visit that place
unannounced, greeted by her.
Feeling free, flying through sunlight
without thoughts of future plans.

Observe the multitude.
What are they vying for?
When it comes, what will it matter?

Is this mine, do I own it?
Has anyone else found this place?
What brought me here?
What keeps me returning?

Someday I may stretch the boundaries,
offer an invitation.
Couch it with the problematic obscurity
and let it mature, ripen, and fall into decay.
The more secretive the more years go by.
Lost appetite for a future,
marked forever as a constant reminder
of everything I have done.

cont'd

Visiting Day ...

Remaining longer with each visit,
establishing a home.
No adventure just stolen imagery,
someday maybe I will move back.

What happened on the way here?
What shaped my destination?
Who was at the wheel?
Was there ever a chance?

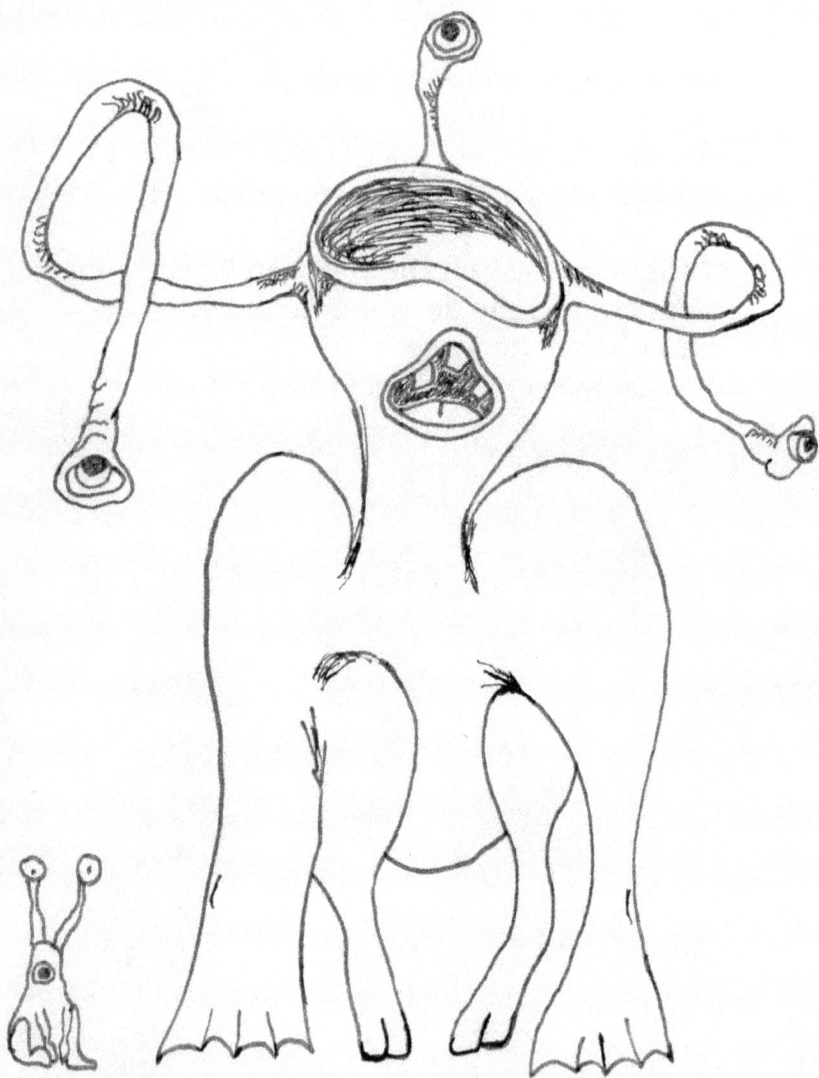

NUMB

I am floating in and out of consciousness,
in and out of sanity, regularly now.
I sit here and can almost feel my isolation bubble thicken.
An exoskeleton forged through detest.
Their voices and sounds muffled in their boring monotony.
Movements appear like shadows scratching across my
landscape.

Each cadaver filled with its own self-importance and place.
Like watching a movie where I'm stationary and everything
goes on around me.

Sometimes I think I should scream out for acceptance.
Upon reflection, the thought of enrolling in their league
makes me nauseous.

I want to run far away from here.
I need to feel accomplishment and worth.
I need to build, to create, to leave a legacy.
I need to know there is a reason.

This day to day existence is too encumbered by minutia,
the flotsam and jetsam of routine.
I have fallen into a hole of mediocrity and acceptance,
continual backfill, growing heavier with every moment that
passes.

RAIN

The rain has come again.
Feels good to wash away the accumulated grime.
The river swells and finds renewed vigour,
continually rising, coming close to breaching its banks,
but it knows its place and levels out at the last moment.

The willows that follow the shoreline, hang and sway in the
breeze.
Sometimes the branches stroke the water's skin,
leaving tiny ripples that manifest downstream.
Each touch changes the river forever.
Other intruders break the surface, insects, cast-offs, detritus,
each leaving its own mark.

A single oak tree and house stand atop a hill as a silent sentry,
while the rain tried to wash away all the years of accumulated
doubt.

Splattered window panes and sodden clapboards
doing their best to offer protection from the outside.
All stained and soaked with the whispers of years gone past.

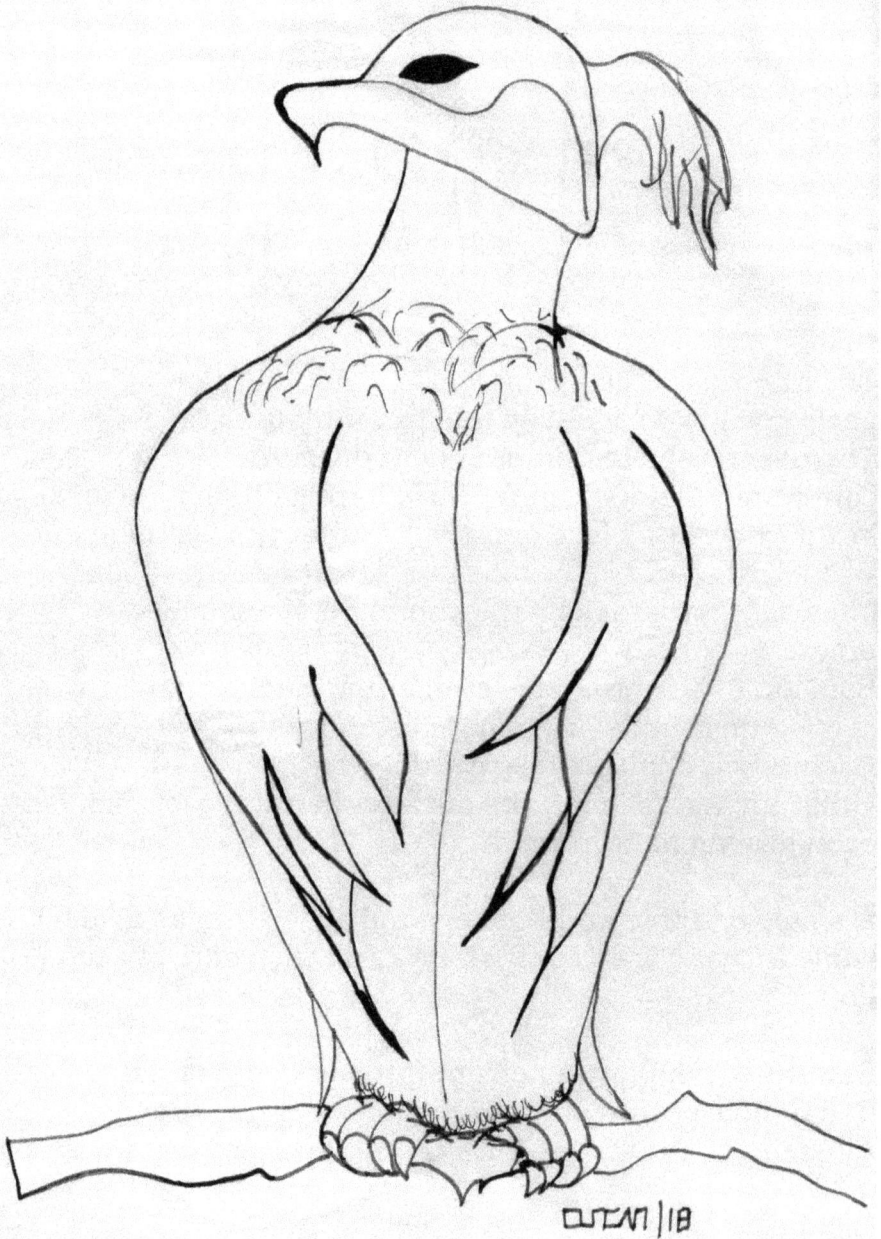

YET ANOTHER GRAY DAY

So, I find myself once again sentenced to a prison term.
How long will it be this time?
Will there be any escape?
I can't see any future now.

Each morning drive is like a walk down death row.
Every day, over and over again,
the same thing; monotony, repetition, automaton; the same.
The scenery through the window never changes.

Nothing in the day to day offers me any joy.
Time is just wasted, what is my contribution?
Does anything I do really matter?
Somebody show me that I make any difference.

Season after season it all blurs and merges into one great
void.
The numbness spreads all over as the ride goes on.
Looking for some kind of meaning, some sign.
What's the point? Why? ... What a waste!

I don't know how much longer I can keep this up,
this meaningless charade.
This grand performance of integration,
this façade of a citizen.

Isolating myself from the surroundings,
limiting any interaction to the bare minimum.
Standing outside of any possible connection.
Keeping my distance and avoiding contamination.

cont'd

Yet Another Gray Day ...

Why can't anyone else see the futility?
Pleasures are found in the most mundane actions.
How could that be fulfilling?
My needs are different, simpler, and less obvious.

My skull aches from inside, I want to scream and shout out.
Desperate to shake of my disillusionment,
begging for some revelation of a purpose,
Some kind of motivation, a glimpse of reason.

What if this is all there is?
Everything just is! There is no reason,
no master plan, nothing
just this.

DAUGHTER

Born to us in love,
you will always fill a special place in our hearts.
Not because you are ours, but
because you are unique.

You constantly amaze us with your
creativity, imagination, sympathy, and individualism.

We cry when you cry,
We laugh when you laugh,
We get angry when you do.
We fall with you,
and fly higher than we ever have, on your wings.

We can see a lot of us in you, but you are not us.
You have many more and varied abilities.
You are a one off, you are you,
And that's what makes you special.

OBSERVING the CAT

Inside the box, outside the box
no one knows if you're alive or not.

When the atom fires
will the hammer swing.

Let's have a look at the cat in the box,
until that time no one knows.

Out of sight, out of mind
you may well be out of time.

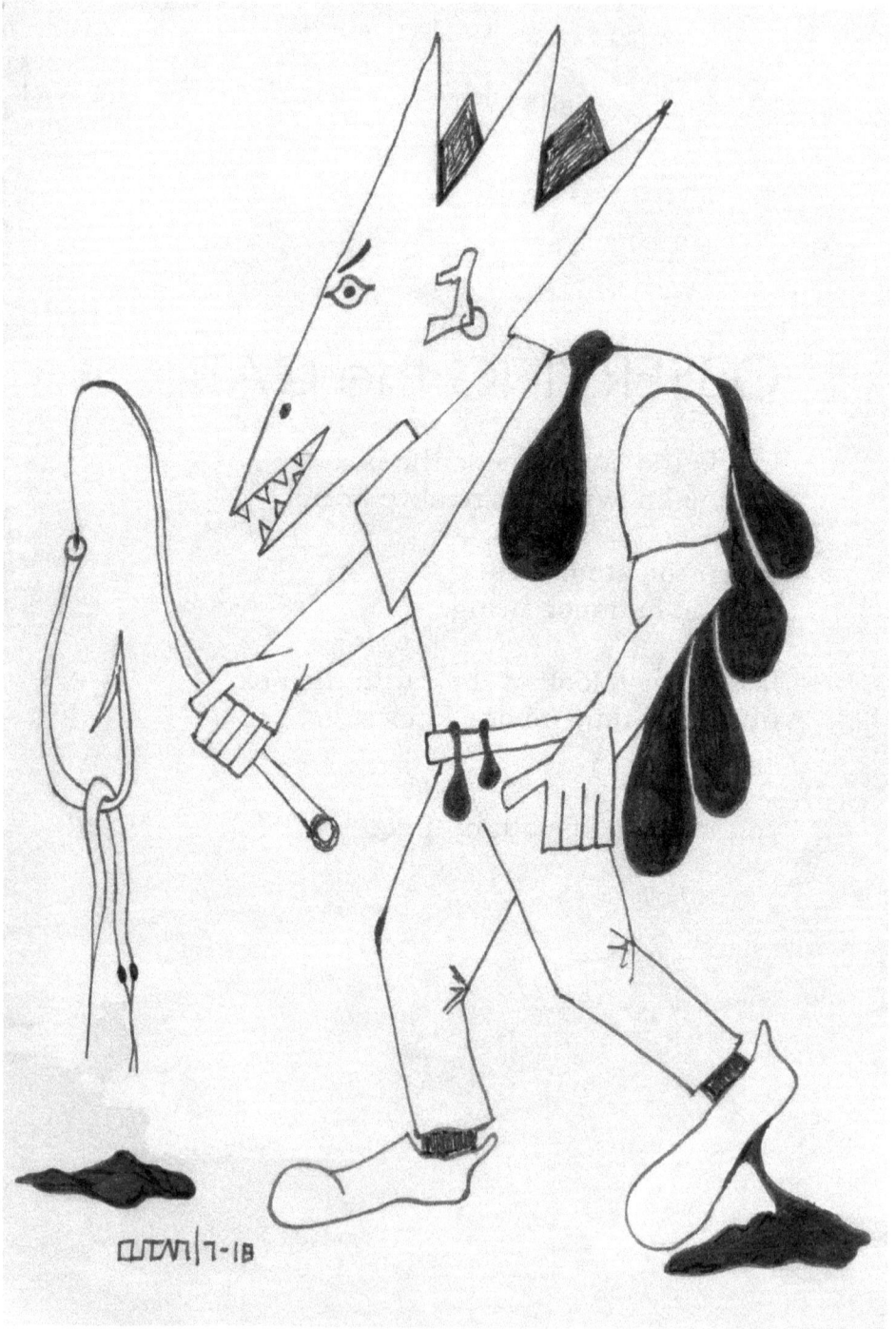

ALSO ON LEAVING

I left a note on the table by the bed.
It took some time to write it,
so, take your time reading it.

I have to leave
someday I'll be back.
When the train leaves the station
and my fate steers me around,
I'll see you again my friend,
out on the edge of town.

Don't ask why
I can't tell you now.
Something broke in me
and I don't know how.

So, save a thought for me.
One day you'll see a sign,
somewhere down the road
you'll see me for the first time.

32

jai garu deva

We lay on the sand together that night.
You said you knew what was to come.
I couldn't see the future quite right
but you said you only saw one.

(chorus) jai garu deva om

The stars and the moon shone oh so bright.
Who could imagine it would all turn out black.
Cause you could always shine some light
but I would always hold back.

(chorus) jai garu deva om

I wish I had known better that time.
So today I wouldn't have to look back.
Cause your light was bright and you tried to show me a sign
and I was unwilling to crack.

(chorus) jai garu deva om

Today I walk down these empty streets at night
and try to hold back a cry.
I know now you had called it right
and this bird just had to fly.

(outro) La la la la la

https://nacnud.bandcamp.com/

SONGS and LYRICS

When I think of what has been
many years go by.
Holding back my silent scream
when you come to say goodbye.

Someday, someday when you're older you'll come back to me,
until then I'll just spend my time, dreaming what could be.
I've spent too much time searching
for what I thought was missing.

Force me down paths of discovery
hoping I may find some sanctuary.
For all the many hard-learned lessons
I'm really left with few impressions.

BOX

I can't suffer this box anymore
rip back the lid, let me out.
I need to wander, I need to be free.
The air within these confines chokes me with every breath.
Dark, meaningless, confinement
chained to unfulfilled dreams.

Cheated from a future that meant something,
a never-ending battle against an internal oppressor.
A nameless, faceless force that whispers of
what could have been.
Constantly tempted and tormented with a carrot of
what should have been.
Time to let go, accept the inevitable and sleep forever,
nothing offers a glimmer of light, a beacon, a meaning.

Crack the darkness, reclaim motivation, shape the
future path push forward and drive through the void.
Look to find something, anything on the other side,
something that would say ... you have a purpose

here it is!

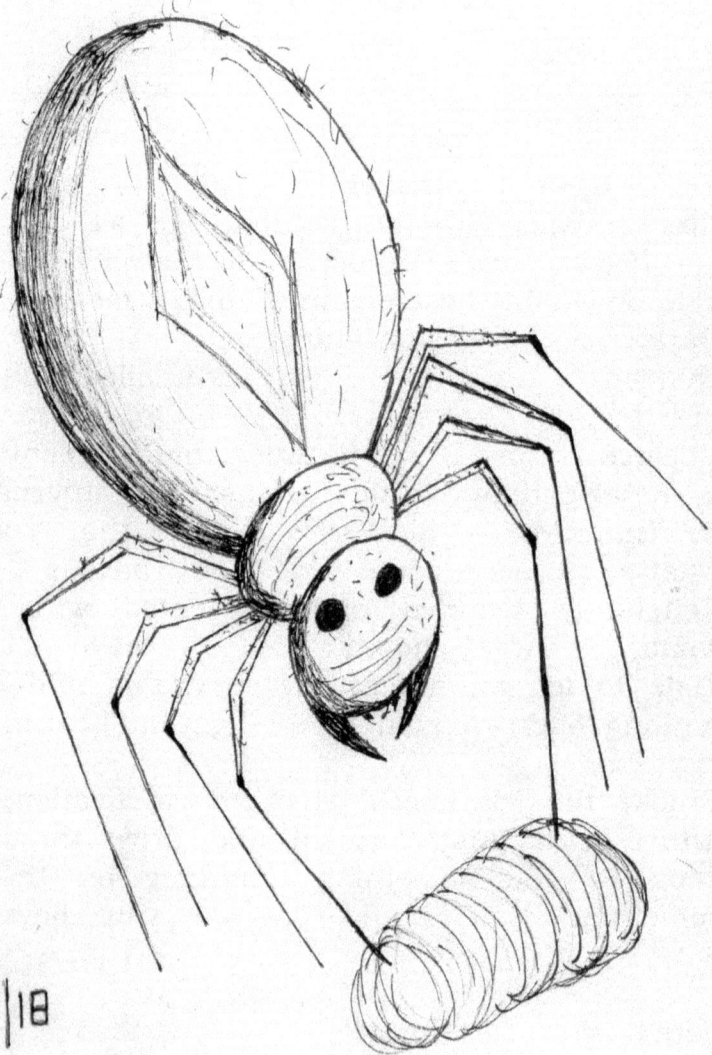

SEPTEMBER

Summer days that seemed to have no end in sight when you were young.
Blue skies splattered with a sampling of cotton ball clouds.

None of us knew what our futures held after that summer, but I think we
all felt that we would have to cut our own path from here on out.

I think there was a realization that the world we were about to enter was a
lot more complicated and unforgiving than the one we were about to leave.

Amanda moved away the following September.
I only saw her once more after that,
about ten years later.

We filled each other in about the missing years.
Talked about the others and where they had ended up.
And as unexpected as our rendezvous was, she left,

and that was that.

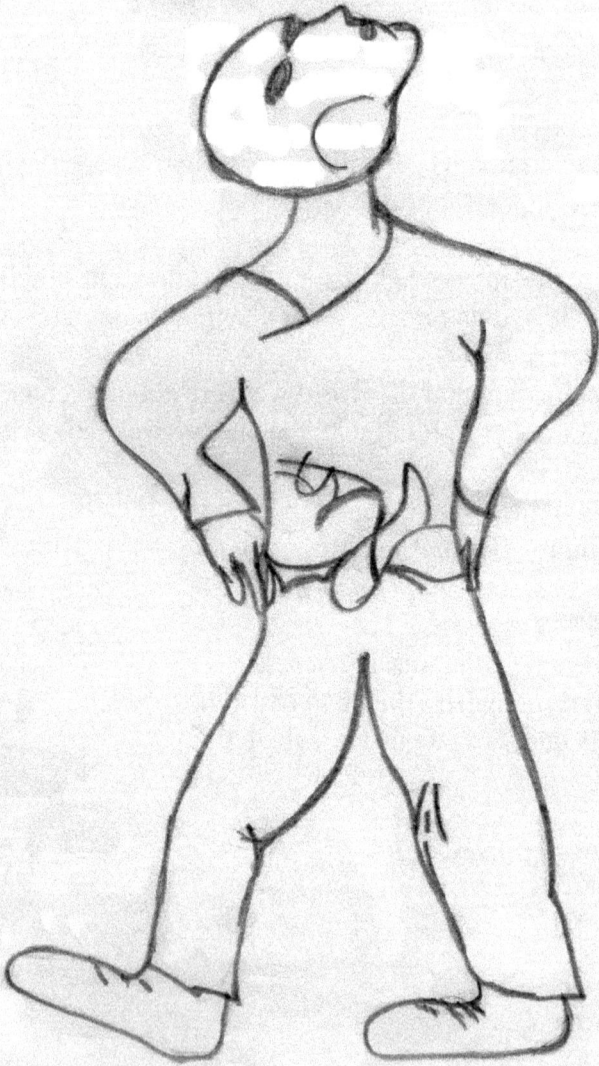

UPON RETURNING[1]

I
Approach through prairie scrub lawn
where tuffs of long straw grass clump together,
stand like islands, in an ocean of detritus
hard packed humus and clay.

Beg to the gods that watch
to conjure up spontaneous storms,
providing the rains that will
wash clean and renew.

II
A long time since I walked this path,
dust covering my boots with each step.
Destination is always the same,
results are always the same.

Onward trek, solitary house on the hill,
well established overrun avenues of approach.
Closed unwelcoming door as portal
breach the boundaries in silent acquiescence.

Square bared wood floor room,
the colour of earth.
Aged tell-tale scratches of continual revisions,
spring renewals and winter retreats.

cont'd

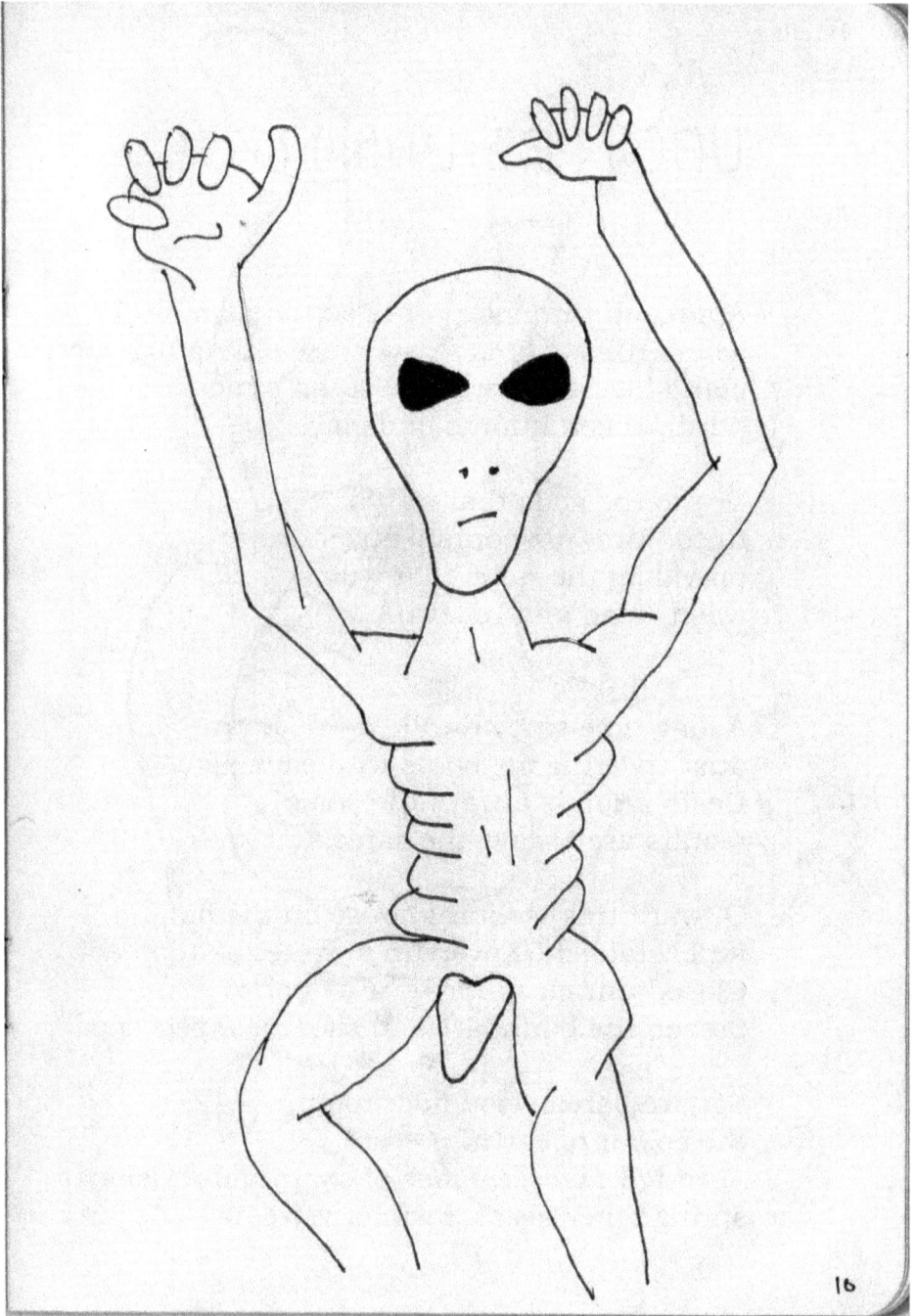

Upon Returning ...

III
Dream washed walls,
layers of hope-filled patterned paper.
Clinging to what might have been
and failing on what was.

Abandoned patterned drapes drawn aside,
four panes of a fogged window revealed.
Mind's eye sentry to the world beyond,
silent witness to what is.

Sunlight streams through between cloud cover
and paints washed out yellow squares on the floor.
Outlines an abandoned plan, while
dust motes collide like ancient galaxy forming
cosmic debris.

White ghost sheets shroud abandoned furniture
each *Cracker Jack* surprise awaits unveiling.
Holding promises to rediscovered memories
and newfound puzzlement.

How do you feel? How do I feel.
I have either suffered from, currently have, or continue to experience

flat feet
osgood shlatters
migranes, high cholesterol, chronic neck pain
deviated septum
Compartment syndrome, Less than perfect vision
Not to mention the lesser
mouth ulcers
acid stomach. ⎤— and self diagnosed but most surely a case of tintinitus.
hemorroids. ⎦
So ask me ~~one~~ one more time ~~again~~ how I feel.
and I will tell you,...
Fine
Now pass me ~~the~~ bottle,
and don't ask again!

                    can
            someone ~~past~~ offer me
Direction, ~~I need~~ Direction —
② pulling a compass from my pocket
   it ~~that~~ spins ~~continually~~ constantly steadily clockwise.
   appearing to keep time rather than direction.
   usless, I offer it to the river with a toss

This has all happened before, and will happen again.
Sleep now, rest and dream.   strange things journeys
dream of magic, distant places, ~~meaning~~, existence and destinations.
Sleep now, soon it will be time to wake.

FEELING

How do I feel?
... How do you feel?

I have either suffered from, currently have, or continue to
suffer from;
flat feet,
Osgood Schlatters,
migraines,
high cholesterol,
chronic neck pain,
deviated septum,
compartment syndrome,
less than perfect vision,
Gilbert's syndrome,
self-diagnosed and now officially confirmed Tinnitus,
hearing loss,
Osteoporosis.

Not to mention the lesser;
mouth ulcers,
acid stomach,
plantar warts,
hemorrhoids.

      Pause.

And now cancer.

So, go ahead and ask me one more time how I feel
and I will tell you, ...

               fine.

Now pass me the bottle and don't ask again.

Parked beneath the hydro tower
Drank a coffee
The towers hum kept tempo with the
    pulsing in my forehead.
Electric, static, hair on my neck and
    arms sticking up.
Air smelled like ozone.
and let the lights glowed dull and
    cat's eye yellow through the fog
absolutely harmless power.
a city's life blood coursing coursing through
    wires
Large monsterous metallic framed skeletons.

[180.00]

WEDNESDAY
UNDER
the
TOWER

I am parked beneath the hydro towers,

large monstrous metal framed skeletons, skinless.

Drinking coffee.

The hum of the wires keeps tempo with the
      pulsing in my forehead.

Electric and static, the hair on my neck and arms begins
to rise.

The air smells of ozone,

and the parking lot lights glow dull and cat's-eye yellow
through the fog.

Absolute un-harnessable power.

A city's lifeblood coursing through wires.

the
sitting
spoken
poetry
man

What foul wind did blow you to my place.
A black night that burns its blackness like dark black skies.

How do you feel in those tights of darkness?

You may be a dragon spitting foam and snot
come to collect what's owed, have you not.

I have walked miles upon the cobblestones that hobble me.

Many lads have legs to beat me.

Deliver cakes unto me, so I may eat the hollow skulls.

What you think you may see, is just what you see.

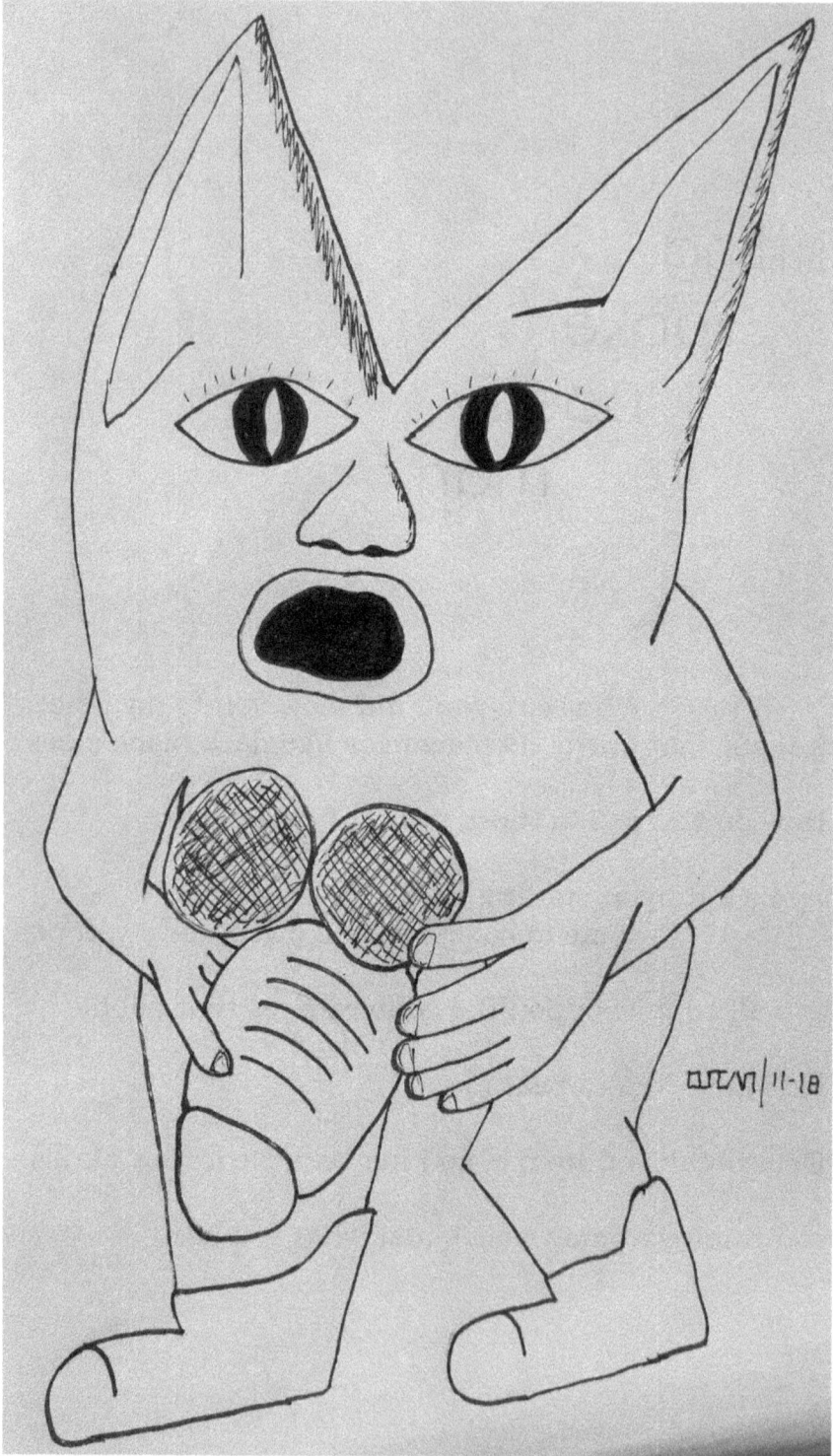

(untitled fragment 2)

I used to do a bit of charity,
for the girls in their new blue jeans
when the truth would not allow us to capture
and would not ever set them free.
How I moaned and cried when
they showed me the truth,
as I crawled through the city at night.

While boys in their bright shiny sports cars
all painted red, silver, and gold.
Drive up and down the high street
remembering their little girl smiles
and grin as they reminisce,
receding memories of a subjective past.

Sunday morning again, I roll over,
birds chime out mercilessly beyond my window.
I have still not got used to this feeling,
or place.

While brown suntanned boys
poke sharp sticks at something,
a lump of blood matted fur
in the middle of this dirt road.

If I could show you my scars, I would,
but they are not visible.
They are mine and hidden
but just as inhibiting.

cont'd

untitled fragment 2 ...

Where were you when I was tired and lonely?
The past is over now, forgotten,
do you want my head?

Wait, there's a noise.
Whispering seeps under the doorway.
"Who's there?"
"What do you want?"
"Why are you here?"

It's getting to the point where I can feel again.

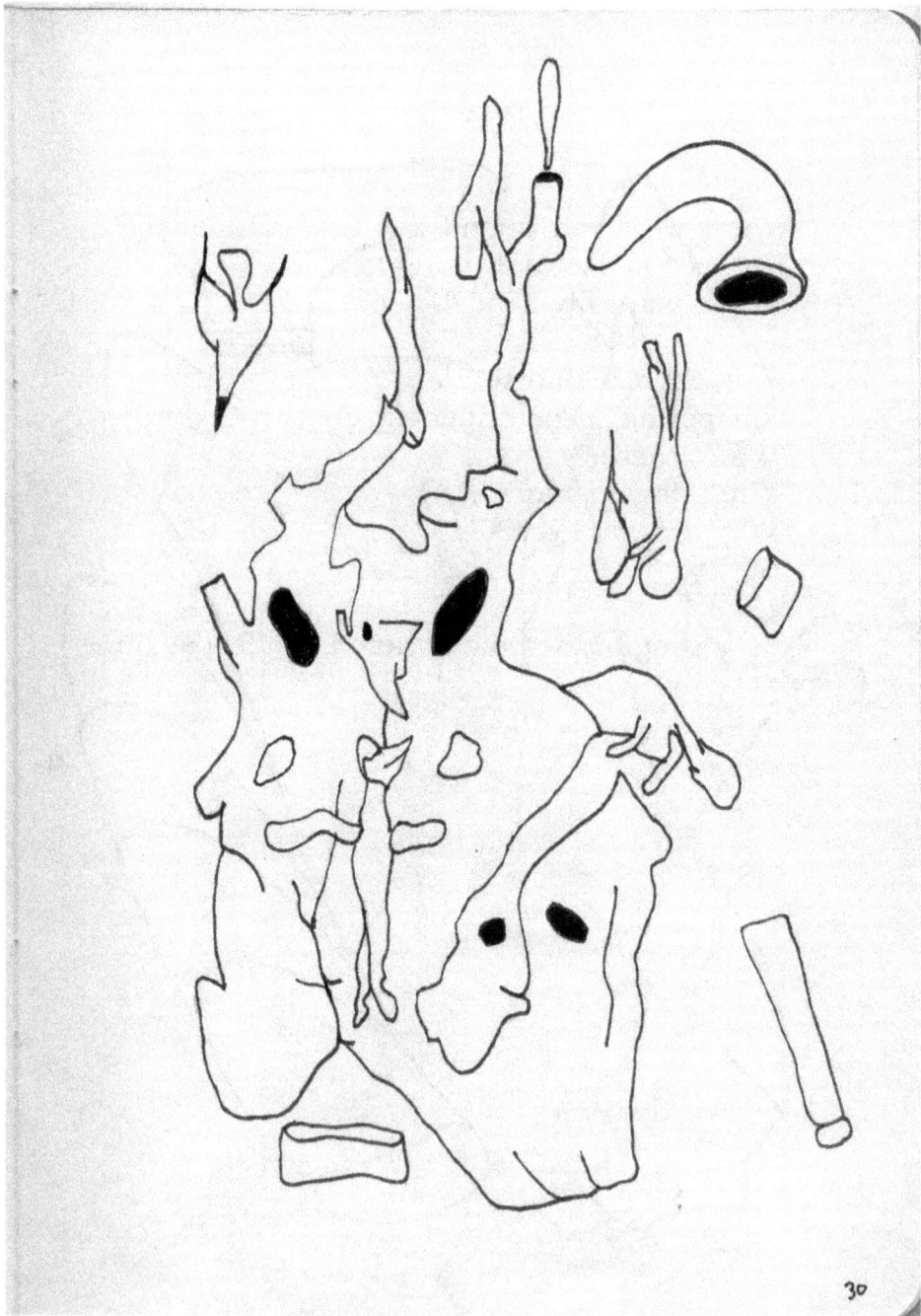

ALSO UPON RETURNING

I

The house still looks the same.
I spent some years wandering,
searching for something, I'm still not quite sure what.
The more I journeyed, the more I became confused,
nothing was clear, nothing was ... revelation.

II

Here I am again, in the same footholds,
staring at the house I left behind.
The house and all it held,
moved on, but still the same.

III

I hesitate to knock, to disturb what's inside.
What would I summon to the door?
Would anyone recognize me now?
Would I recognize anyone beyond this threshold?

IV

What things I must have missed.
What things I have lost.
What things have changed?
What things have remained the same?

A conspiracy theorist suspicious cantrail
splits the sky from a distant silver white
plane.

as a dragonfly, natures hellcycle buzzes my drink

Soft sounds filtering through my ~~blurred out perception~~
Senses.

as. The fog gradually ~~turning~~ burns off the lake.

|
|

mortared field stone fences and privett hedges
delineate the far off fields
cutting out private little sections.

___

How long has it been since I left the machine
Its cogs and gears churning, twisting, crushing, the life out
turning,
spitting out chunks of crap. chewed up hopes and dreams.
plasma and fodder for the weak
How long has it been?
How long has it been since you left me?
Broken, hollowed, beaten and suffering

LANSA Version 11.4
Printed   9/06/01 15:23:39
Partition   DEV——Development Partition

Process   : Bill's stuff
Function   : 0144H4 ——— new bit for o144104
Sequence   129
Label
Command   DISPLAY
MSGTEXT   Message Text

Scholastic Canada
Screen Panel Image

A   78   0   LABEL   5   INP Y Y

SIMPLE BLUE RAIN

A conspiracy theorist's suspicious contrail

    from a distant silver white plane, splits the sky.

Closer, a dragonfly, nature's helicopter, buzzes past my drink.

Soft sounds filtering through my blurred-out deadened senses,

    as the fog gradually burns off the lake.

The sun is on the rise.

Mortared field-stone fences and privet hedges

    delineate sections of the distant hills,

    cutting out private little parts.

Irregular jig-saw pieces welded together.

Together they reveal the bigger picture.

cont'd

Simple Blue Rain ...

Magical in its essence, but in need of an explanation.

Why would such things matter, only in this instance?

My vantage point, distant, and on high, melts into obscurity.

Where the sky meets the land, anything is possible.

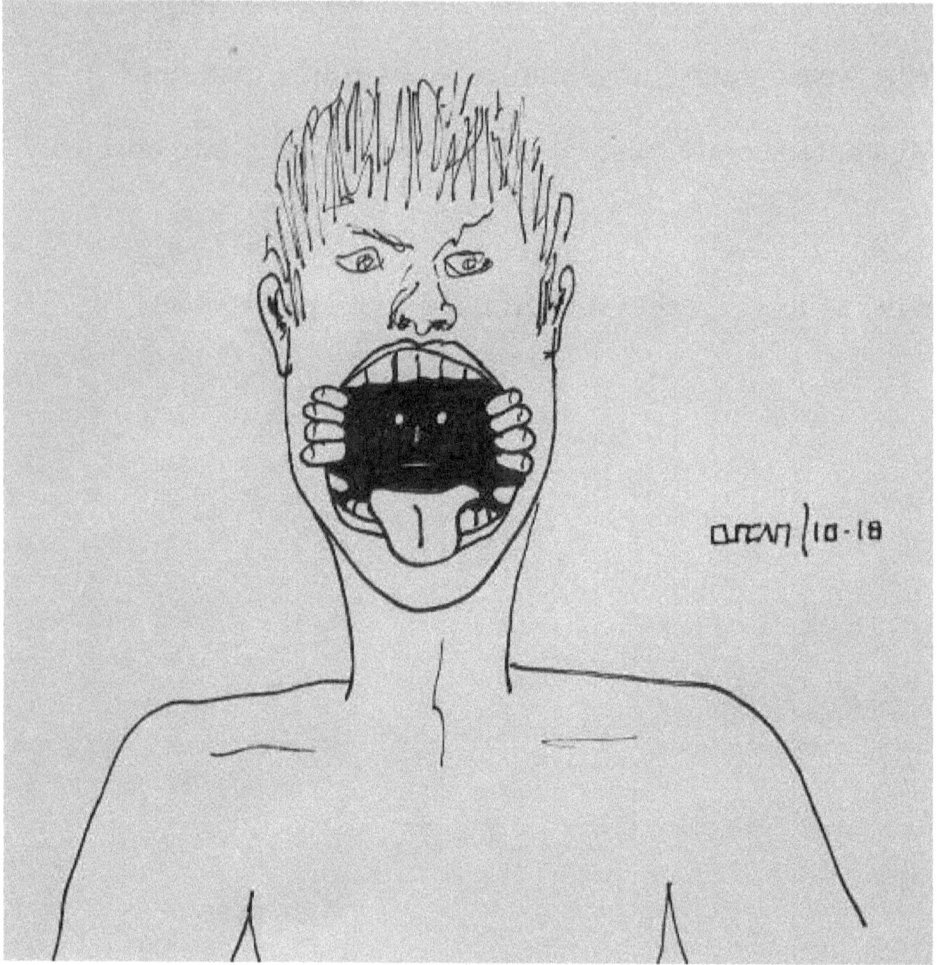

HOW LONG?

How long has it been since I left the machine?
Its cogs and gears, turning, churning, twisting,
crushing, the life out.

Spitting out chunks of crap, chewed up hopes and dreams.

Plasma and fodder for the weak,
Pablum silver spoon fed.

How long has it been?

How long has it been since you left me?
Broken, hollowed out, beaten, and suffering.

How long has it been?

How much longer can I wait?
What is the point of waiting?

I believe I have reached my expiry date.

The green and grey gun metal clouds of yesterday
had given way to the monochromatic grey haze of
today.

The sun a pale washed out egg yoke
posied 20 degrees above the horizon
clearing the tree tops on the far shore
doing its best to burn through the moisture.

water on the lake, still and unblemished
looking like
reflective and smooth as wind swept ice
water, trees, and sky combine as forming a flattened tableau.

An occasional loon call, fish splash, a bird chirp
Filters through breaking the acoustic white noise in my ears
drawing attention away from the internal conversation in my head.
a glass for the more refined
[another bottle, and I should be well and truly on my way]

The wind orchestrates a natural ballet as it
ruffles and sways the leaves and branches of the
distant trees
The Cicadas produce their rhythmic revelry
a natural tinitus
All blend into a cacophony of noise matching the
flog of the day.

a facade for the day

— July 2013

```
*Creation time :  15:23:39
*Creation date :  09/06/01
*Job system name :  SCHCA400
*Copy number :  100
*File number :  000002
*File name :  QSYSPRT
*Time :  15:23:38
*Date :  09/06/01
*Job number :  468321
*User name :  WND
*Job name :  U0000178
```

SITTING by the LAKE

The green and gunmetal gray clouds of yesterday,
have given way to the monochromatic gray haze of today.

The sun, a pale washed out egg yolk,
poised twenty degrees above the horizon.
Clearing the treetops on the far shore,
doing its best to burn through the moisture.

Water on the lake, reflective and unblemished,
still and smooth as windswept ice.
Water, trees, and sky, combine and form a two-dimensional
flattened tableau,
a facade for the day.

An occasional Loon call, fish splash, or birdsong, filters
through.
Water lapping against the stony shore, all provide acoustic
white noise for my ears.
All this draws attention away from the conversation in my
head.

The wind orchestrates a natural ballet
as it pushes and sways the leaves and branches of the
distant trees.

Cicadas producing their ubiquitous sound of fall, a natural
tinnitus,
all blend into a numbing cacophony of sound,
complementing the haze of the day.

Another bottle, or a glass for the more refined,
and I should be well and truly on my way.

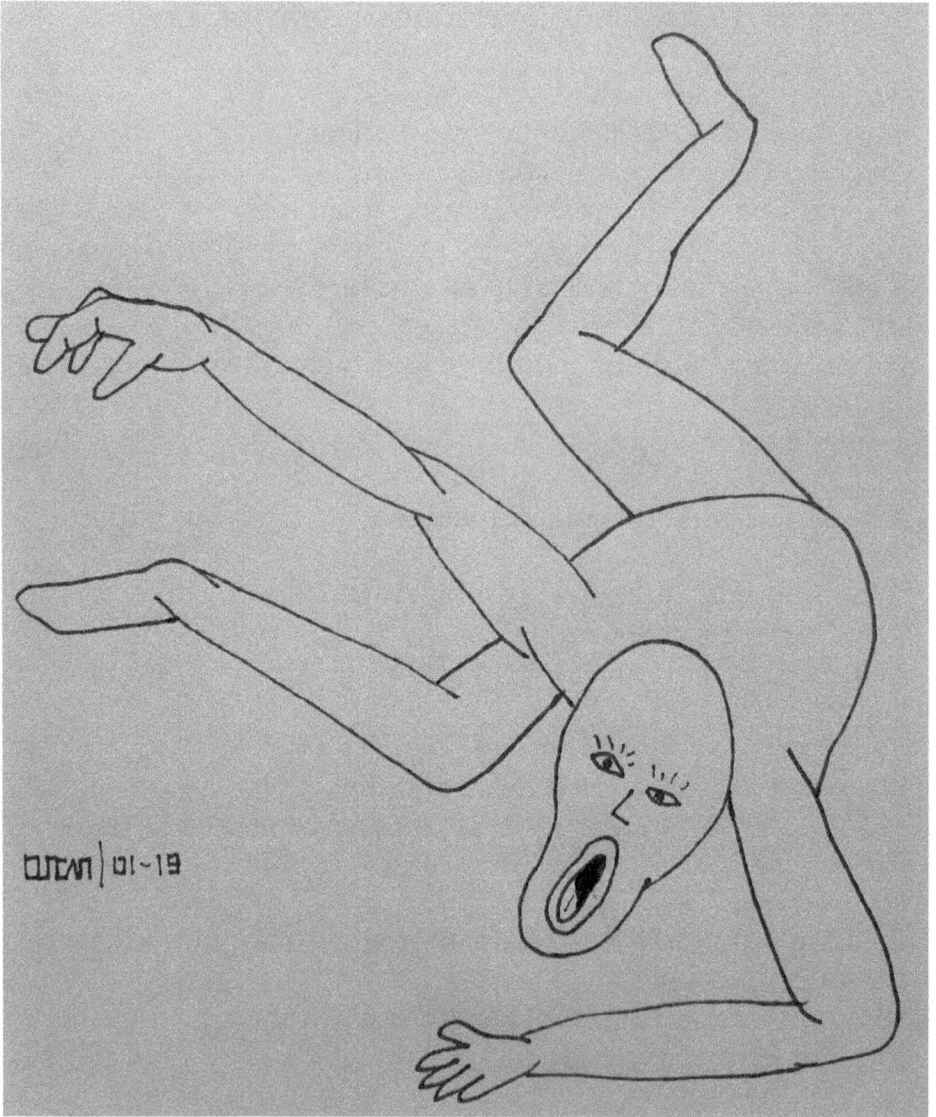

BABYLON

A treasure is buried here, but not beneath the ground.
The third eye diamond waiting to be found.

Nights around the table
while the fires burned brightly,
across these lands
and through time.
We've raised a glass of wine,
forever and for ever.

I wonder how you're sleeping with your new-found friend,
Babble on.

Over the rainbow
we follow our dreams,
wanderers throughout the ages,

in Babylon

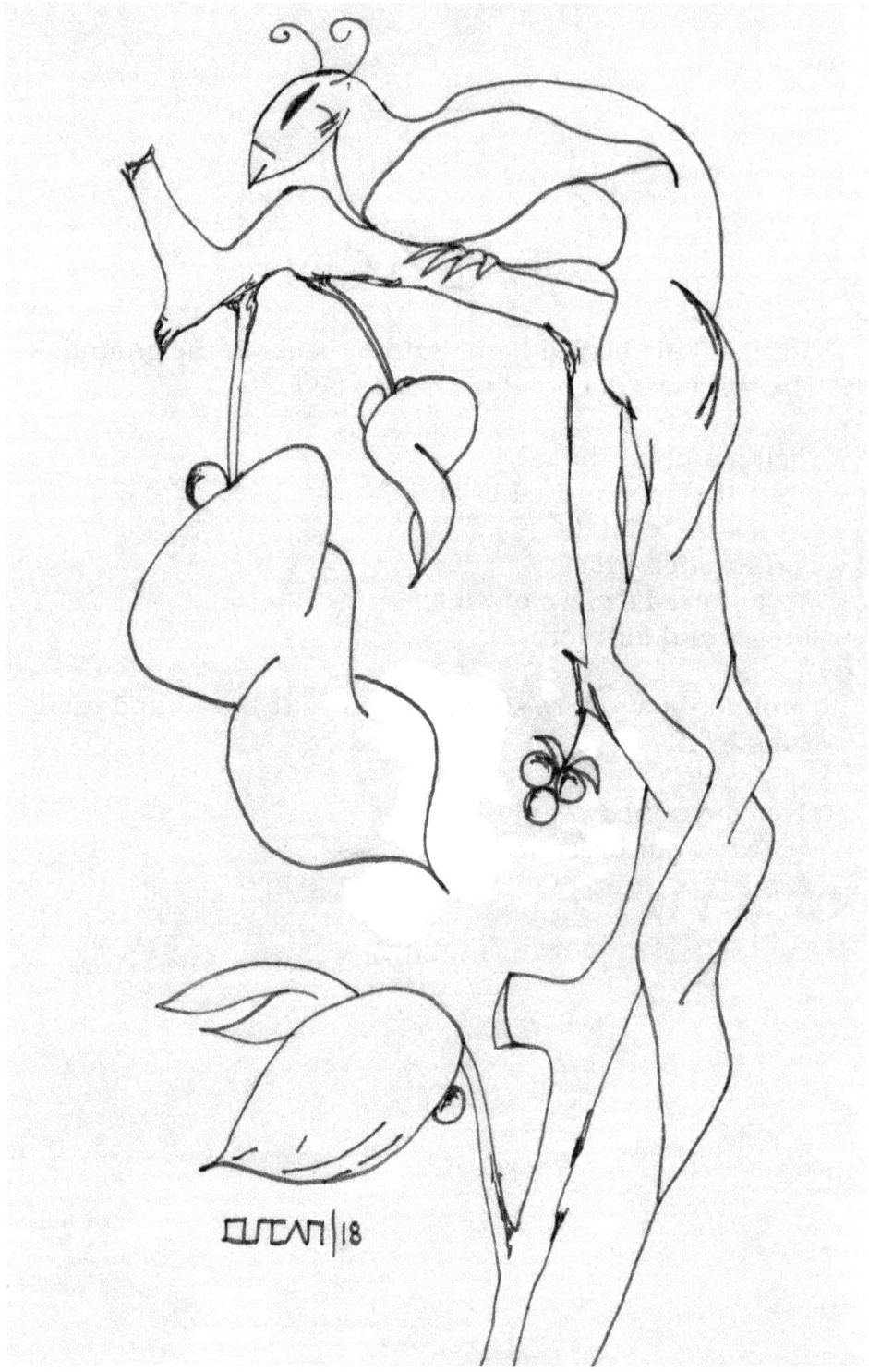

CRAWL

Crawling through the fog and haze of everyday existence.
Learning the daily drudge by rote.
I feel myself slipping ... drifting in and out.

Some part is missing, a hole takes its place.
Filled with emptiness and darkness.

Something essential to the machine has been misplaced.
Something required to give this meaning,
some reason for existing, some reason for being.

Constantly seeking answers to questions unspoken.
Released from the incessant dialogue in my head to the
ether,
with hopes that some divine manifestation will reward me
with answers.

Every day now, I feel like I'm in a daze,
the endless drone of life,
routines, unwavering and constant in their monotony.
Searching for some meaning, some reason to continue,
feelings brought upon not by melancholy but by boredom.
What kind of a waste is this short time here?
What reason do I have to continue?

Here I am.   Dec 13/17
Step up, pick a line, any one.

"You, yes you, go to that line."

me, "which line? This one?"

An angry finger points me over there, to a different line

Step forward, wait, step forward, wait.

Red Sign flashes, WAIT.

Step forward, wait, step forward, wait.

Sign turns green, ENTER.

I'm next to go through the door.

"Hey you, move over to that other line."

"What, now?" Again I have to move.

Move to the end of a new line

Step forward, wait, step forward, wait.

Red Sign flashes, WAIT.

"Hey you. Move back to the previous line."

"you've got to be kidding me."

LINE UP

Here I am,

Step up, pick a line, any line.

      "You, yes you, go into that other line."

Me, "Which line? This one?"

Angry finger waves me over there, to a different line.

      Step forward, wait, step forward, wait.

Red sign flashes, *WAIT.*

      Step forward, wait, step forward, wait.

Sign turns green, flashes, *ENTER.*

I'm next to go through the door.

      "Hey, you. Move over to that other line."

"What, now?" Again I have to move.

Move to the end of the new line.

      Step forward, wait, step forward, wait.

Red sign flashes, *WAIT.*

cont'd

Line Up ...

"Hey, you. Move back to the previous line."

You've got to be kidding me.

"You gotta be kidding me."

"Please Sir, if you would. What is your number?"

"Number, what number?"

"Did you not take a number when you arrived?"

"No, I didn't know I had to, no one said anything."

"Okay, then you need to go get one and rejoin
the line, please."

"Seriously, you gotta be kidding me."

JAN 4/18   INVASION

Raise up men it is time.
We have been called upon
      to defend our temple, our homeland
      against the invaders.

The place we where we lived and grew, is
now under attack.
      we have a right to defend repel and
obliterate this unwelcomed intruder.

Into Battle now men, this is our land,
no one else will settle here.
      Eliminate this blight completely,
We will Use every option you have to destroy it.
OUR MISSION IS SINGULAR, COMMITTED AND WITH PURPOSE

We will route out the enemy, anywhere
      give him no place to hide.
      Search him out in every street every corner

The enemy invaders will be annihalated utterly destroyed

We will not stop until every vestige of this
foreign abomination has been eradicated

UP, UP, BOYS, IT'S TIME FOR BATTLE

FIGHT HARD BOYS, WE WILL WEAR OUR WOUNDS AND SCARS
      AS MEDALS.

INVASION

"Rise up boys, it's time to engage the enemy.
We have been called upon to defend
our temple, our homeland,
against the invaders.

The place where we live and grow
is now under attack.
We have a right to defend, repel, and
obliterate this unwelcome intruder.

Up now boys, up, it is time for battle.

Into battle now boys, this is our land,
no one else will settle here.
Eliminate this blight completely.
Use every option you have, to destroy it.

Our mission is singular, committed and with purpose.
We will rout out the enemy anywhere he hides.
Give him no place to shelter.
Search for him on every street and every corner.

The invaders will be annihilated, utterly destroyed.
We will not stop until every vestige of this
foreign abomination has been eradicated.

Fight hard men, afterwards, we will
wear our wounds and scars like medals."

AN IMAGINED LIFE   JAN/18

IT'S OVER NOW YOU SAID (Remarked)
OUR EXPERIMENT, OUR COLLABORATION, OUR PARTNERSHIP.
OUR DOWNTOWN / BARN RENTAL

SCENES THAT PLAYED OUT OVER THE LAST YEARS
RAINY INDOOR EVENINGS, SPLATTERED PATTERS ON
        THE WINDOW

SUNNY SUMMER SUNDY MORNINGS, LAYING IN BED.
BLOWING WINTER STORMS, WHILE BUNDLED TOGETHER
        Reclined on the couch, watching through the window as the
snowfell   THROUGH THE POWER OUTAGES, & APPLIANCE FAILURES

WHAT DO WE DO NOW?,
WHAT DO WE DO WITH THIS... DATA?

THIS COLLECTION OF FEELINGS, HAS BECOME MORE
WE MADE MEMORRIES.
These don't fade, they dont disappear, they manifest
they mean something. they have value.

But NOW WE PART, We separate, we are
to go our own ways new
Some where down the line there will be a
            Reconcilliation.

IF THEN ELSE

It's over now, you said.
Here it is, the end of our experiment,
our collaboration, our partnership,
The downtown one bedroom apartment in the centre of the city.

Scenes that played out over the last few years.
Rainy indoor evenings, wet splattered patterns on the windows.
Blowing winter storms raged outside,
while we were bundled inside together by the fire.
Reclined on the couch while watching through the window as the snow fell.
Soldiering on through the power outages and appliance failures.
Walking the downtown streets at night in the rain.
Waking Sunday morning and lying in bed until noon.

What do we do now?
What do we do with this … data.

This collection of feelings, the accumulated bulk of a relationship,
has been transformed into memories, we have ... history now.
These don't fade, they don't disappear, they manifest,
They mean something, they have … value.

But now we part, we separate, we are to go our separate ways.
Somewhere down the road, there may be a reconciliation,
but we both know the chance of this happening is slim at best,
better to accommodate each other and prepare for the next adventure.

You were the first one, you were the last one.

Pain   MAY 28/18

Slow dull *minutous* throb,
That's how it comes on at first
Waits there, (beating)(Pulsing)(throbing)
until you decide to breathe

Then hard solid hammer thump
Bang, Bang to your insides
A cold steel sledghammer smack
Someone wants attention

Movement is out of the question
To my position, The slightest accomodating adjustment
          and you get the knife thrust
through ~~to the~~ the centre of its existence.

                    fundamental
Try some ~~substantial~~ rearanging of self
and it will let you know, who's Boss
Hot wires will radiate from it's core.
Growing larger as they spider leg out

Nothing works to ease the pain.
Let it play out, curse it ~~aloud~~ out loud
It will reel itself back in,
until you ~~decide to~~ wake it once more
          inadvertantly
          unintentionally
          reluctantly

PAIN

Slow dull monotonous pulsing.
That's how it comes on at first.
Waits there throbbing,
until you decide to breathe.

Then hard solid hammer thumps.
Bang, bang on your insides.
A cold steel sledgehammer smack.
Someone wants attention.

Movement is out of the question.
The slightest accommodating adjustment to my position,
and you get the knife thrust,
through to the centre of its existence.

Try some fundamental rearranging of self,
and it will let you know who's the Boss.
Hot wires will radiate from its core,
growing larger as they spider-leg out.

Nothing works to ease the pain.
Let it play out, curse it out loud.
It will reel itself back in,
until you reluctantly wake it once more.

Sə Sept 27/18

Black Goo

coils
roils

What black slime crawls around inside me?
Churns, and bubbles, scratching at new paths
Looking for any breach, grab a new foothold.

Hollowed out crap holes, invader of destruction
Shells of usless, mis.informed, baggage.

Claws bared looking for purchase.
Grabbing and mauling, scratching and tearing
Finding a way out.

Putrid, uncalled for, unwanted, undesired,
    form of punishment

Black multilegged programmed insect of destruction
Predator with no sense of goal, no ultimate desire.

Genetically designed to destroy its allotment
and move on.

this invader
What possible use does it have? This scourge should
be completely and forever intilated.

BLACK GOO

What black goo crawls around inside me?
Churns and roils, scratching out new paths.
Looking for any breach to grab a new foothold.

Hollowed out crap-holes of destruction.
Shells of useless, misinformed, baggage.

Claws bared looking for purchase.
Grabbing and mauling, scratching and tearing,
looking to find a way out.

Putrid, uncalled for, unwanted, and undesired slime.
Some form of punishment for crimes unknown.

A black multilegged programmed insect of destruction.
A predator with no sense of direction, no ultimate goal.

Genetically designed to destroy its allotment
and them move on.

What possible use does this invader have?
This scourge should be forever and completely annihilated.

Here be

Bonus Material

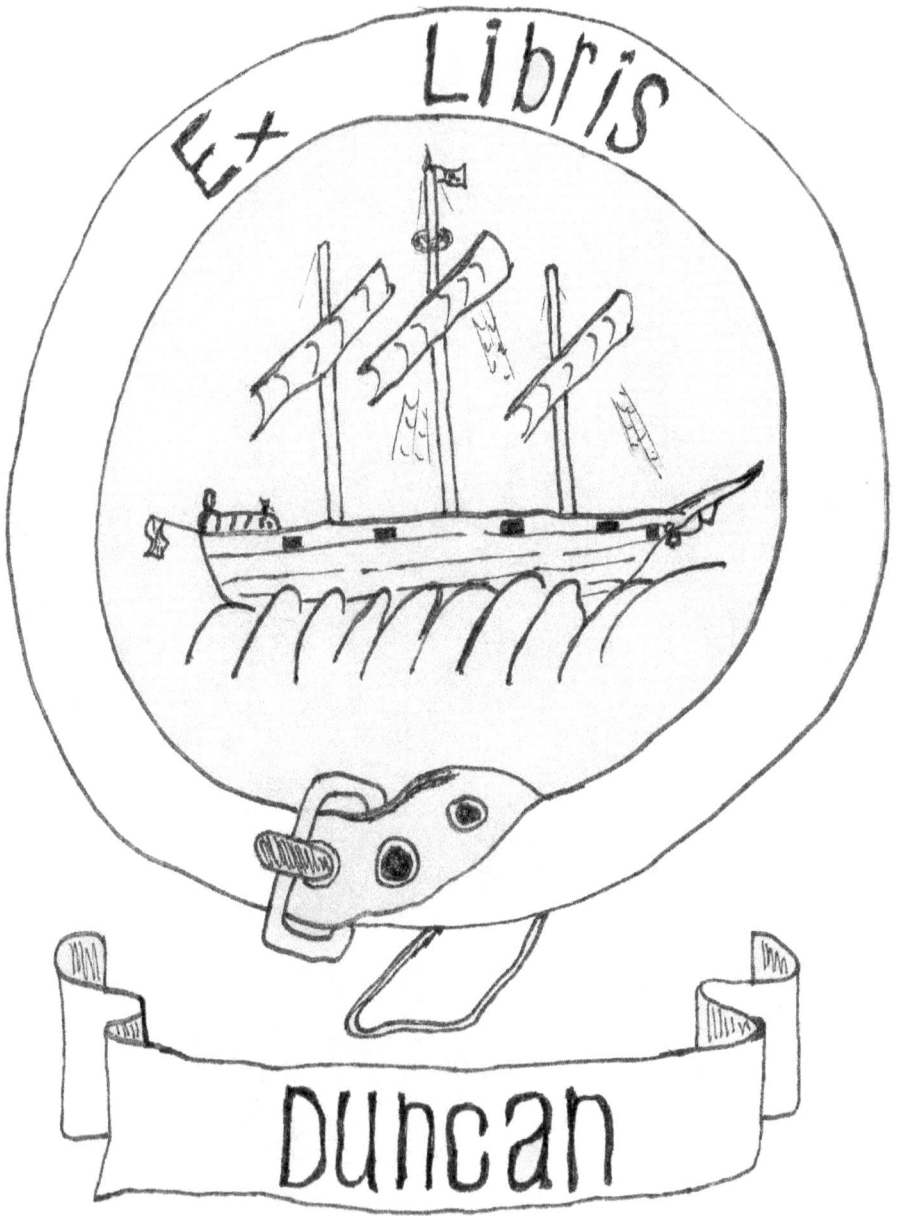

Ex Libris

Duncan

A Script

Nautonnier

by

William Duncan

End sequence only, Un-produced draft

<u>END SEQUENCE</u>

FADE IN:

1   EXT. BEACH - SUNSET   1

LONG SHOT

Tropical island beach, water to one side, sand in the middle
and trees and forest on the other side. Looking along the
beach camera starts to travel over the sand. Centered
shimmering out of focus image in the distance grows larger
as view moves in. Image comes into focus and reveals a man.
DAVE sits on the beach looking out at the sun setting over
the ocean. BILL approaches from the side.

ZOOM IN

                BILL
      Can I sit?

Dave stares straight ahead, gestures with his right hand to
a place on the beach beside him.

PAN TO FRONT

                DAVE
      Why did you come here today?

                BILL
      I thought maybe I could accomplish
      something.

                DAVE
      Like what? (a beat) What do you
      mean?

                BILL
      I got this weird feeling that
      something is going to happen.
      Something wonderful, something I
      need to be part of, (a beat)
      witness.

                DAVE
      Where do you need to be?

                BILL
      I haven't arrived yet.

A beat.

                          (CONTINUED)

                    DAVE
          What do you mean?

                    BILL
          Depends. For me it means I am not
          happy. I am not comfortable with
          where I find myself at this point
          in my life. Especially career and
          personally. I feel there is more
          and I have not found it yet. I am
          not happy with my current lot.

                    DAVE
          Will you ever be?

                    BILL
          Don't really know, but I know how I
          feel now and if I ever get there (a
          beat) maybe (another beat) I hope I
          will feel differently, like I'll
          have some sense of accomplishment,
          that it was all worthwhile somehow.

A blinding flash of light starts at point on horizon where
the sun was setting and spreads out to the edges. A few
seconds of ripping sound then no sound, soundtrack is silent
for remainder of spreading light.

                                        FADE TO WHITE:

                    WOMAN(V.O.)
          This has all happened before, and
          it will happen again.

MONTAGE

-- first initial single cell life form dividing up

-- sea life

-- something crawling along the shore

-- lizard crawls in a tree

-- flock of birds takes to the sky

-- first primitive ape men in trees (on desert savanna)

-- primitive human pushes up from the dust and dirt and
starts to walk erect.

END MONTAGE

                                        (CONTINUED)

                                        FADE TO BLACK:

                    BABY(V.O.)
                  (crying)
              Crying

                                        HARD CUT TO:

2   BEGIN CREDIT ROLL   2

        Scroll end-credits over downtown scene of a large city.
        Audio should be city sounds (traffic, horns, parks, school
        yards, kids, barkers, voices, general cacophony of city
        soundscape)

        END CREDIT ROLL

                                        FADE OUT:

                    THE END

A Comic

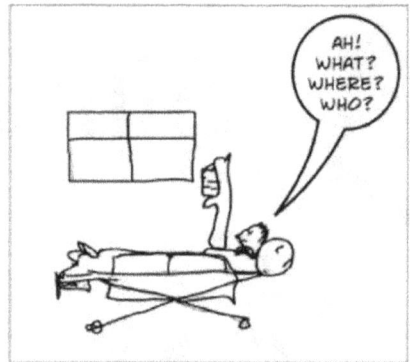

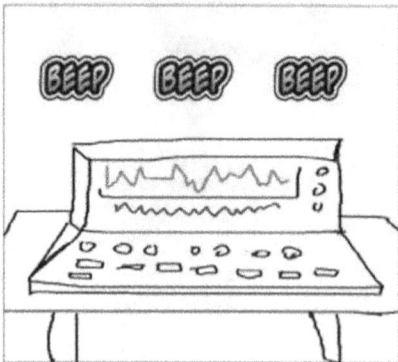
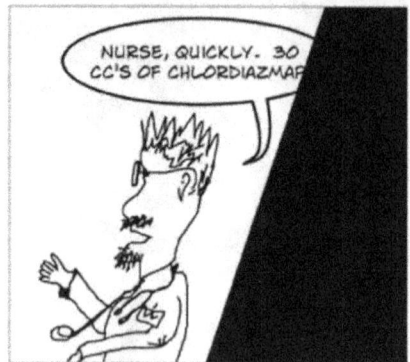

Copyright © 2014 by duncan

1

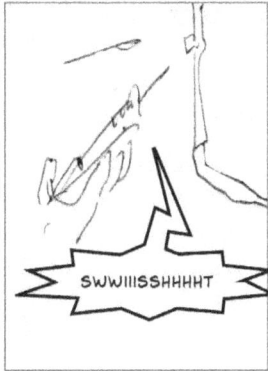
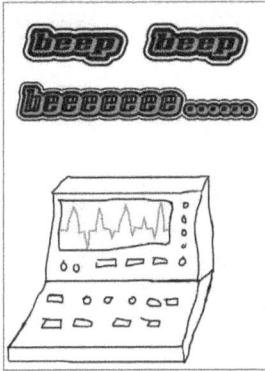

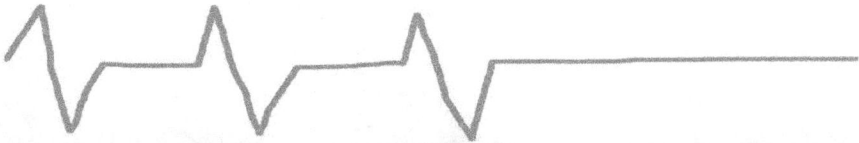

4

5

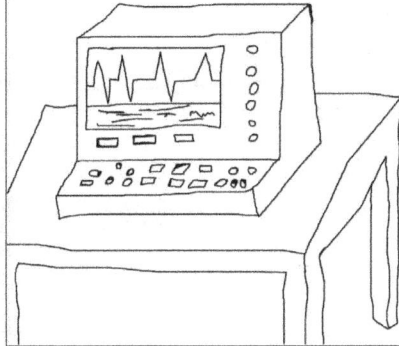

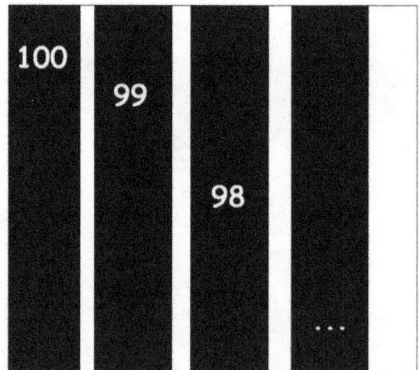

7

Murcalumis

* comic book back cover

Notes, Study Guide / Remarques, Guide d'étude:

1: On Leaving, House, Upon Returning; they form an unintended trilogy. (pp 9, 17, 49)

2: Similar themes are explored in the poem Image (p13) and the comic Simulacrum. As well as the overall theme of the book.

3: Poems Rain (p29) and Upon Returning (p49); are they the same house?

4: Most common and repeated themes, symbols, and subject matter to explore.

- Water/Coast
- Leaving/Travel
- House/Home
- Train
- Seclusion/loneliness
- Questions
- The Quest
- Puppetmaster

- Meaning of Life
- Boredom/Monotony
- Sounds in the Head
- Machines
- Fatalism
- Discomfort/Pain
- Surreal imagery

_____

_____

_____

_____

_____

_____

www.ingramcontent.com/pod-product-compliance
Lightning Source LLC
Chambersburg PA
CBHW020552030426
42337CB00013B/1064